PASSIONATE LIFE

NIKITA MAHAJAN

This book, Passionate Life, is dedicated to everyone who dares to follow their passions and dreams. It is for those who are prepared to take chances and put forth the effort necessary to realise their most improbable dreams.

Anyone who aspires to build something greater and more audacious than themselves. It is for those who are prepared to take a chance, trust their instincts, and accomplish the improbable. It is for those who put in a lot of effort, never give up, and never lose faith in themselves.

People who get back up after failing and keep going; for people who don't let setbacks keep them from accomplishing their objectives. Finally, this book is for everyone who makes a difference in the world and inspires others.

I hope you all have the fortitude to face the world and lead passionate lives.

Contents

Contents

Preface

Welcome to **Passionate Life**, a book that draws from the experiences of real people to assist you in developing a virtuous and moral outlook on life.

Everybody has goals, aspirations, and dreams. But frequently, life challenges can make it hard to accomplish these objectives. Many of us experience self-doubt and feel we are not reaching our full potential at times.

You can use this book as a roadmap to help you navigate those challenges and better understand who you are. It will assist you in developing a solid and satisfying relationship with yourself and realising your true passion and goal in life.

You'll find motivational tales that will assist you in connecting with your true self and passions throughout the book. Additionally, you'll discover how to strengthen your character, gain more self-assurance, and discover your life's purpose.

It is designed to assist you in taking control of yourself and realising all of your potency. You can live an ardent life that is filled with joy and reason if you have the right perspective and the right resources.

So let's embark on our journey to a brand-new, optimistic you. Let's learn to appreciate every minute and live passionately. It's the moment to design a happy and fulfilling life.

PREFACE

Let's make *Passionate Life* a reality!

Acknowledgements

I want to extend my sincere gratitude and appreciation to everyone who helped make this book, Passionate Life, a reality.

.

First and foremost, I want to acknowledge my family, kohinoors and pupils who have supported me, even when my ideologies have seemed impossible or outlandish. I am appreciative of their unwavering love and assistance during this journey.

.

I also want to express my gratitude to the publishing house's staff for their efforts, support, and advice in seeing this book through to completion. The group played a key role in creating a high-quality product, from the editor to the InDesign.

.

Finally, I want to express my gratitude to all the readers who gave this book a chance because they thought its message and the efficacy of positive thinking would be worth it. Your bravery in placing your faith in my opinions and insights has encouraged me to keep expressing my viewpoint to people worldwide.

About The Author

Nikita Mahajan is an experienced research scholar and content writer from India. She is the author of two books, Caged Memories (2021) and Shamanic Flame (2022), published under her pen name Inky Niks. She is passionate about exploring the depths of knowledge and advocates for understanding beyond the worldly realms.

She aims to inspire readers to reflect in-depth and have meaningful conversations. She respects the value of connecting with one's soul and the influence of knowledge. She wants to give readers a chance to broaden their horizons and gain a deeper knowledge of themselves through her writing.

It is sufficient to say that Nikita Mahajan is a genuine scholar and writer who is deeply committed to education, comprehension, and introspection. Her books are a testament to her commitment to and love of literature.

ONE

APPRECIATE YOUR ATTITUDE

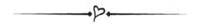

Once upon a time, a girl lived in an urban town. She had a lot of friends, and she loved to spend time with them. She was always energetic and delighted, and everyone adored her.

One day, she lost everything. She wasn't sure what to do next because she didn't have any money or support that could get her another life. Her family has left her struggling, too, as they didn't have enough for their kids.

The girl was depressed about how bad things were getting and turned on, sobbing all the time. She didn't wish to go on living like this anymore!

The girl tried to accept her by saying things like "everything has changed" or "things got better." Soon those things made her feel very fortunate! She sluggishly stopped crying until one day, she said something like:

You have a lot to be appreciative of. You have the freedom to decide on and agree on what you wish to do with your life and how you choose to live it.

You are self-sufficient in the stringent regulations that ensure others from walking ahead in their lives.

You can decide how much money you spend, how much duration you spend working, and how much time you spend with your family.

You have been provided with so many blessings in this realm; it's virtually unthinkable to comprehend all that you've prevailed upon until you commence seizing notice of them!

If you allow yourself to appreciate your attitude, you'll be surrounded by glorious twilight and dawnings, the people who encircle you, and even your own body, soul, and mind. You will always discover something unique to be grateful for every day.

ϷϷϷ

TWO

BLISS IS ALWAYS BELIEVABLE

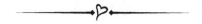

That's right, it's true! You heard it right!

The sun had just begun to set on the horizon when a young boy Bliss lost his parents at a very young age. He had no idea where his life would take him; he knew he had to make his way into the world.

He decided to use his last bit of courage and wander off to find his destiny. He walked until he reached a place he had never seen before. It was a beautiful meadow surrounded by tall trees, with a stream running through it. He told himself that when this stream wasn't flowing, the same old water when the tree wasn't holding the same old leaves, why was he making everyone gloomy?

After experiencing the struggle, somehow, he got a job unmatched by his qualifications!

On Friday evening, he was sitting on a couch at home, just gawking at the calendar hanging on the wall. As he glimpsed the date, he thought: "It's Friday. It can't be happening."

He had been promoted to supervisor, and entities were getting on well despite the growth. At the same time, he decided to quit his job. He started searching for employment and gave interviews. Well enough that his life had come with an abrupt twist, due to which he started dwelling here and there. But then, all of a sudden, something hit him: There's no job made for him!

He ceased every aspect of life, bowing his head —no questions asked. And when his sister found out what had happened, she assisted his decision.

Those Twenty-five days and nights, he stayed up late thinking about ways to find the best days. He laughed and joked about himself that his life had played out well. And then he nodded off with visions of being able to get one job. Everything seemed perfect to him in his eyes.

It's a straightforward concept—you must reckon that you can accomplish your purposes and visions. That's it.

There's a secret: most people don't think they achieve their goals and objectives. And so they don't because they're too busy doubting themselves and their abilities.

But Bliss didn't do that! He knew that he could do ANYTHING. If you also put your psyche to it (and believe in your Bliss). Everyone has seen what happens when people follow through with their plans: they succeed! It's just as simple as that if you want something, go for it! You'll be amazed at what happens when you start believing in yourself (and in us)!

So if you want to get ahead in life? Then stop wasting time wondering whether or not things will happen for you—take action! Start small and build toward bigger goals every day until your dreams come true!

ᐅᐅᐅ

THREE

Conquer The Challenges

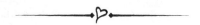

A tiny Mantis was strolling through the woods. It found itself where it didn't anticipate what to do or say. The tiny Mantis decided to talk to an old tree for assistance.

It asked the tree if it knew how to conquer the challenges.

While reverting, the old tree said: "The first challenge is that you don't know where you are going and where you are coming from.

The second challenge is that you don't have anything" After paying attention to this, the tiny Mantis got unhappy because it didn't know how to conquer those challenges.

Then, an Eagle heard the Mantis' painful voice and yearned to help. So the Eagle said:

"The first challenge is that you don't know where and where you are coming from.

The second challenge is that you don't have anything."

After noticing this, the tiny Mantis got happy because it understood its problems and how it could solve them.

The first phase to acknowledging your hurdles is knowing them. You must take a moment to honestly look at what you are encountering instead of just guessing or discussing it.

Once you've spotted a challenge, the following step is to choose a plan of action to conquer it. It can be as thorough as pleading for support from others or taking on unique entertainment, but it should be powerful and effective if it's going to boost you to move ahead in life.

Always come up with a plan for conquering your obstacle, and put yourself up for attainment by shrouding yourself with optimistic thoughts that can aid your endeavours and help to counsel you along the path!

ᐁᐁᐁ

FOUR

DIVE INTO YOUR DREAMS

A girl who lived her dream when she was in seventh, everyone demotivated her, but she never lost hope.

She dreamed of cracking a competitive exam. She did dare to work hard for it. She wanted to be a doctor, but she was tortured and harassed because of her surroundings. She tried so hard to crack the paper.

Every day she skipped her morning prayer and studied with the assistance of one of her best teachers. Others commented in thirty minutes what she could achieve.

Finally, the day came when her heart started pitter-patter. She had no idea there was something better waiting for her just around the corner.

She was happy and a little down at the exact moment with what she had achieved so far in life, but she still couldn't imagine getting honoured by those who dragged her faith down.

She understood the value of diving deep into her dreams; she could do anything.

You also have to believe in yourself and put your compassion into it. You know that nothing is perfect, but you also know that you can't let that deter you from aiming to enrich your soul. If there's something you wish to acquire, get on it!

You might not be able to fulfil everything immediately, but that doesn't mean you should cede to your dreams. It will work if you keep striving until you ultimately get where you need to be. Never let others tell you differently!

FIVE

EMPOWER YOUR ENERGY

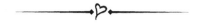

Being a child, Cyril was always told to try harder. But he didn't know how to do it. He felt like his energy had been weakened, and he couldn't do anything with it.

He was always told to study hard for school and get good grades. But he didn't know how to look or what studying was.

His parents wanted him to get on a path that would lead him toward success, but he was unaware of finding his true self.

Those around him were telling him that if only he had done this, then maybe things would be different. But there was no way for them to show him how because they didn't know either! In high school, he became more aware that no one around him empowered their energy.

He first begins by lifting his energy. Although it sounds simple, it is! Everyone concentrates on the adverse aspects of life and forgets about the positive. You shouldn't wish to be happy—you must work on yourself!

If you're not focused on yourself and your demands, it makes it simple for others to decide for you. If you don't take care of yourself, others will benefit from that certainty to support themselves.

Ultimately, learn to pardon yourself for any perceived injustices to move forth without clasping onto pessimistic sentiments from the past (or present).

ᗞᗞᗞ

SIX

FOCUS ON FAITHFULNESS

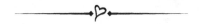

Once upon a time, there was a young man named Max who was struggling with his studies. He had tried different techniques and strategies, but nothing seemed to work. He had begun to give up hope when one day, he heard a wise old man say, "Focus with faithfulness."

Max was intrigued by this phrase, and so he decided to try it out. He began to focus on each task that he had to do and put in total effort and concentration. As he continued to concentrate with faithfulness, he found that he could achieve much more. Not only was he able to complete tasks faster, but he also began to see results that he had never thought possible.

Max was amazed at the difference that focusing on faithfulness had made to his life. He began to tell his friends and family about it, and soon more and more people were asking him for advice. Max was proud of the difference he was making and determined to continue focusing faithfully on everything he did.

Max's story reminds us that, with focus and faithfulness, we can make a difference. We can achieve results that we never thought possible. So, let's get out there and make a difference by focusing on faithfulness.

You have so much to offer so much potential! And you'll live your life to the fullest because that's what you want.

ᵖᵖᵖ

SEVEN

GLORY OF
GRATITUDE

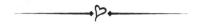

Once upon a time, there was a young prince named Abeer. He was a brave and kindhearted man who always sought ways to help those in need.

One day, while Abeer was scouring the kingdom, he stumbled upon an older man. He was standing alone, looking sad and forlorn. Abeer asked him what was wrong, and the older man told him his story. He had once been a prosperous merchant, but bad luck had cost him everything.

Abeer felt great compassion for the man, so he chose to help. He offered the older man a job at the castle, assisting with the day-to-day tasks. The older man was very indebted, and he thanked him for his tenderness.

The older man's gratitude extensively moved the prince, motivating him to do more good deeds in the kingdom. He became known as the prince of appreciation, always glaring for ways to alleviate the less fortunate.

His acts of kindness were not forgotten, and the kingdom's people began to look up to him. His story of glory and gratitude spread far and wide, and he became an emblem of faith and mercy to many.

Abeer had taught the kingdom a valuable lesson. Gratitude is an essential part of life and can bring glory to those who embrace it.

ᗮᗮᗮ

EIGHT

HARMONIOUS HOPE

Harmonious Hope had longed for harmony for years, ever since she was a small child. Every morning she'd wake up and hope that the day would bring peace and tranquillity, but every night she'd go to bed feeling as if her dreams were out of reach.

As the years passed, Harmonious Hope grew older, yet her hopes and dreams of harmony were never realised. She knew she had to take matters into her own hands if she wanted the peace she longed for.

She concluded to take a voyage in the exploration of harmony. She wandered far and wide, digging for answers. Everywhere she moved, she implored the same question: How can I bring peace to my life? She didn't get any response.

She was so tired and found herself in a place where everybody was doing their chore. She sat on a mounted rock, gazing at a bird sitting peacefully on the stem of an old tree without any leaves, where she became invisible to everyone.

After searching, Harmonious Hope finally found what she was gawking for. She realised that true harmony was seen within one's self. She comprehended that she had to let go of the anger, hurt, and pain she held in her heart and restore these adverse emotions with devotion, acknowledgement, and endorsement.

With this newfound knowledge, Harmonious Hope subsided at home and concentrated on nurturing harmony within herself and her environment. Over time, she started to feel the peace she had longed for.

Harmonious Hope had finally found her longed-for harmony. Her excursion was complete. She had found out that true peace could not be found in the outside world but could be created from within.

ᐅᐅᐅ

NINE

INTEGRITY IS IMMORTAL

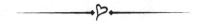

Aeons ago, there was a province ruled by a Queen. She was a fair and dedicated leader, but she had one fault: She was tormented by her power and hegemony. She speculated that he was an extensively noteworthy person and that no one could disregard him.

One day, as she sat on her throne in her mansion, an old lady said: "You are not the most valuable person in this world; you are only one person out of many."

The queen was amazed by her statements and demanded to know who this woman dared contradict her. The old woman replied: "I am an immortal. I have been alive thousands of years and will live for thousands more."

The queen was angry when she heeded this because she had spent her whole life struggling to prove herself worthy of greatness and now that woman had come along and told her that she didn't deserve any of it!

But then the old woman spoke again: "Your superiority is nothing about what I have," she said. "You believe you can control me? You do not infer what ability I carry within me."

The older woman said she would explain it to her!

When you think of integrity, what comes to mind? A person with a strong sense of honour and contentment? A person who won't alter their beliefs for anything? A person who exists by their word and doesn't fabricate? Is someone trustworthy and reliable?

Well, those people don't exist.

There's a reason why integrity is immortal: because it's not about being precise. It's about being TRUE. It's about honouring yourself, even if you make blunders or do things that aren't right. You can still be yourself even when you're not performing the right thing. You can still be ethical and honest with yourself when others aren't telling the truth."

ᗡᗡᗡ

TEN

JOY JUMBLES

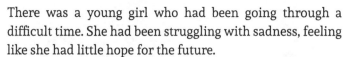

There was a young girl who had been going through a difficult time. She had been struggling with sadness, feeling like she had little hope for the future.

One day, she decided to take a walk to clear her head. As she walked, she noticed a small stream of water, and the glimmer of something in the water caught her eye. She bent down to take a closer look and realised that it was a small goldfish. She picked it up and was mesmerised by its beauty.

Suddenly, a sense of joy washed over her. She felt like a huge burden had been lifted off of her shoulders. She realised that pleasure could be found in even the smallest of things.

From then on, she made a conscious effort to look for joy in everything. In the beauty of the sunrise and sunset, in the laughter of a child, in the kindness of a stranger, in the calmness of a lake. She found joy in the good and the bad moments in life, making everything more bearable.

She eventually learned to embrace the joys of life and stopped letting the hardships get her down. She knew that happiness was indeed in everything.

ϷϷϷ

ELEVEN

KINDLE IN KINDNESS

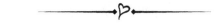

There once existed a small village by the sea where the folks were kind and thoughtful to one another. Everyone in the townlet laboured together to make it a delightful place.

The day passed, and one day a stranger arrived in the village. He needed help, so the townies greeted him with open arms. They took him in and provided him with food, shelter and apparel.

The stranger was astonished at the mercy of the villagers and yearned to pay them back in some way. He thought of a way that he could kindle kindness in the village. He decided to start a small garden in the village yard.

He would plant numerous flowers and vegetables in the garden and care for them daily. He would also entice the townies to come and enjoy the garden and share in the beauty of nature.

The stranger's kindness encouraged the villagers. They began to show more compassion to each other and their neighbours. They would support each other with duties and share resources. They even began to share meals and tales in the village yard.

The stranger's kindness spread throughout the village, and everyone felt powerful as a community. The stranger had ignited in turn, and it had made a difference.

The stranger moved on to another village, but the people of the small town never forgot the kindness he had shown them. They continued to be kind and generous to each other and their neighbours. They learned that kindness could make a difference and be kindled in many ways.

One of the most important lessons of all: is that kindness is the most powerful tool anyone could ever possess.

ᗡᗡᗡ

TWELVE

LEAD WITH LOVE TO LEARN

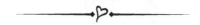

Down memory lane, there was a young man who was so ambitious and driven that he could not halt himself from trying to lead. He wished so badly to be the best leader that he could be.

But what did he do? He went out into his town and started leading. And it didn't work out so well for him.

He threw his weight around in meetings, but people didn't listen because they knew he was trying to take over the company. He gave inspirational speeches, but people didn't even know what to listen for because this guy wasn't all that bright or charismatic.

And then, one day, the young man realised: maybe I should just be myself!

That's better than trying to be someone else—and besides, if I'm not pretending to be someone else, then maybe people will listen when I speak up!

And then they did! And they listened more than ever before!

So learn from this story; don't try too hard to be a leader! Be yourself and let others join you in your leadership journey!

ᗐᗐᗐ

THIRTEEN

MOTIVATION IS MOVEMENT

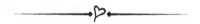

The day Ridhaan realised he was a vessel for all the people telling him to move up and do something was the best day of my life.

He was sitting in my cubicle in a job he didn't want, but he felt he had no choice but to hold onto it. It was a typical first job experience:

- The boss was a nightmare
- The work environment was toxic
- There were too many rules

But then something happened: he looked around the office. He realised that everyone else was doing it because they thought they had to—because it was what they were supposed to do or because it seemed like their parents expected them to do it, or because they preferred to fit in with their companions who did it. None of those justifications felt like they amounted to anyone at all.

He once felt his motivation was more consequential than anyone else's even if other people thought otherwise. And so, when his boss told him he needed some new software that he wanted to write overnight so that he could show off his latest project at an upcoming conference, he started digging into it.

In the beginning, there was nothing. And then, there was motivation.

Motivation is the force that drives him to do things and achieve goals that are beyond what he could have ever visualised. It is the fire that burns in the belly of every human being, and it's how they make their rut through life.

But motivation can be fleeting as short-lived as a candle flame or as potent as an atomic bomb. Courage is like a butterfly: sometimes it flickers around for a while, then wrecks into a barrier and dies.

Through his life experience, we can ensure how important it is to keep our flame burning bright. If we live by this story of his life, when our motivation flutters away from us again, we'll be able to pick it up and start again with something new because we all need inspiration now and then!

ᗞᗞᗞ

FOURTEEN

NOW

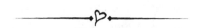

Last year around this time, a man lived with many issues. He struggled to find purpose and meaning, was dissatisfied with his occupation, and did not get along with his wife.

He decided to take charge of his life and make changes someday. His way of thinking was "ability is always now." He began daily meditation and reading spirituality-related books.

After a while, he realised that he couldn't just snap his fingers and make everything better overnight—he could choose how things would go from this point forward.

His quest for self-mastery thus began as he discovered how to live in the present and stop letting regrets from the past or tense relationships prevent him from living fully and freely in any given moment.

His friends began to worry about him when they noticed that he wasn't smiling as much anymore, but after some time had elapsed and they realised how much happier and more fulfilled he was than before, they realised why it was so crucial for him to find his path to true happiness.

He heard a voice that spoke to him. It said, "The most powerful thing you can do with your life is never to stop.

Stop being afraid of being an idiot, stop trying to be perfect, and start. Stop worrying about what other people think of you and be you. Never stop learning, but never stop growing. Stop trying to control every aspect of your life and let go of it all."

He was taken aback by these words, and he knew this was the answer he was looking for. He had the strength to take a leap of virtue and bring in some changes in his life. He began to take risks and challenge himself. He stopped trying to please everyone and started living his life according to his terms. He embraced adventure and allowed himself to grow.

His life rewrote drastically, and he soon lived a life full of joy and passion. He was no longer a victim of his occurrences instead, a producer of his destiny. He had found peace and balance and was ready to take on the world.

He had finally learnt never to stop and listen to the voice within himself. He had learnt to trust his instincts and take the path that was right for him. He was ready to take the world by storm, and he knew his life would never be the same again.

FIFTEEN

OBSTACLES ARE OPPORTUNITIES

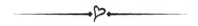

You know that old saying, "Obstacles are opportunities"?

It was a typical summer morning, and the sun was shining brightly. Alice was at her window, gazing out into the surroundings with a deep sense of longing. She liked to analyse and feel everything spirit had to deliver, but she was too fearful of taking any risks.

She had grown up in the suburbs and had never left it. Fear of the mysteries had kept her from venturing out, but she had an internal passion for glimpsing and discerning new quirks.

One day, Alice decided to seize an opportunity and embark on a journey. She had no indication where she was going, but she was deduced to make the most out of it.

On her journey, she confronted many obstacles. She had to uncover paths to withstand them, which wasn't susceptible. But, she was kindled to keep going and eventually found herself in unfamiliar yet exhilarating places.

To her surprise, she discovered that these obstacles were opportunities. Through her experiences, she learned more about herself and the world than she ever could have inferred. Eventually, she realised that the hazards she took were worth the reward.

Her journey was a life-changing ordeal, and she had come to appreciate that the world was filled with opportunities.

Later on, she met some pretty intriguing identities. People who have been through some stuff and how they look at life are so different from what she used to see. And then, there are people like her who have been stuck in their little rut for a long time. Internally, she felt that all are looking for something new but don't know how to get there.

Ultimately, she said. *"The world is full of obstacles. It's hard to find a path through them, but it's worth it when you do. Obstacles are opportunities to learn new skills and to adapt."*

▷▷▷

SIXTEEN

PASSION IS POWER

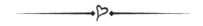

Lily was a young girl born into a middle-class family. On her birth day, everybody shed tears. There was a collective disappointment in the air because it was a girl child. She felt unloved and snubbed by her loved ones.

No one was there to support her or to listen to her concerns. When she made mistakes, her parents scolded her, and her siblings would make negative comments. Her relatives would try to manipulate her thoughts, leaving her feeling helpless and scared. She had lost her childhood innocence and had become frightened of the world around her.

Though she was young, she was incredibly innocent and determined. She knew that she could make a difference in her own life.

Growing up, she realised that she enjoyed her company and loved being alone. She tried to follow her passions, no matter how often she failed. She tried to be strong and never give up on anything.

So, despite the lack of love and attention from her loved ones, she decided to embark on her journey. She wished to make something of herself without proving to anyone that she was more than a forgotten girl.

Lily pushed herself to great lengths, doing things that no one else thought she was capable of. She studied hard and manoeuvred harder. She was passionate about the power to make something of herself and to make a difference.

Soon enough, Lily left everything in divine light, kept doing her deeds and made a name for herself. She was successful, but she still felt like something was missing. Her success did not fill the gap left by the lack of love and attention.

But she was determined to keep going and pushing herself, no matter what. She was adventurous and brave, and she had to make an imprint.

Lily's story reminds us never to give up and to keep pushing ourselves no matter how hard life may seem. No matter how much we may be ignored, we can still make a difference and succeed only if we follow our passion with power.

ϷϷϷ

SEVENTEEN

QUILLING AWARENESS

Susan was a girl who lived in the Urban Town. She had a lot of talent and creativity. She enjoyed making things and trying new things. She learned about the new craft of one day. She was very curious and eager to give it a try.

Susan chose to go to a quilling class. She was astounded by the gorgeous artwork that had been produced using only paper and glue. The amount of detail and how exquisite the creations could be gobsmacked her. She even mastered the art of 3D objects.

Sarah was motivated to develop her quilling venture after the training session. She wished to raise awareness of quilling and the artwork it was possible to produce. She decided to compile working with different designs into a collage and document the process online. To persuade individuals to participate in the discussion, she also made a tagline for it.

Many people joined the discussion and began appreciating the beauty of quilling due to Susan's efforts. She was incredibly pleased with herself for raising awareness of the craft. She left an enduring appearance and contributed to the overall enjoyment.

It accounts for how Susan's awareness of quilling left a profound impact and inspired many people to pursue it.

ᐯᐯᐯ

EIGHTEEN

RESILIENT RIGHTNESS

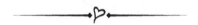

There once was a large, sturdy tree in a far-off forest that stood tall and proud. The tree had faced many challenges throughout its life, including ferocious winds, rain, and snow.

The tree, however, persisted in doing what was right in every circumstance.

Unexpectedly, a storm drifted through the woods one day, abandoning a path of devastation. The massive tree branches were torn off by the wind, which was also strong enough to uproot the tree.

The tree was alone and helpless as it lay there.

Days went by, and the tree gradually recovered as its branches and roots began to expand. The tree was adamant about rising and being proud once more. But the tree still had a lot of obstacles to overcome.

The vegetation struggled against the adverse weather and the constantly expanding dandelions threatening to engulf its assets. But the tree persisted in breaking through impossible odds. It inevitably attained standing back in awe once more.

The tree had succeeded in overcoming every challenge and emerging stronger. It had adhered to Resilient Rightness and regained its proper position in the forest.

Regardless of how difficult the circumstances were, the tree had taught everyone that as long as one chooses resilient rightness, nothing is unachievable.

The tree served as a source of inspiration for everyone and demonstrated that, despite hardships, it is essential to maintain strength and adhere to moral principles.

ᚦᚦᚦ

NINETEEN
Solace in Smiling Silence

The sun was setting behind the snow-covered Himalayas, painting the sky in a million colours as the boy sat atop the hills of a little village of Himachal. The air was so still and peaceful, unlike the of the city.

The young boy had grown up in the serene, beautiful hills of Himachal Pradesh. The lush green forests and the glorious mountains dotted with wildflowers, were a perfect backdrop for his preadolescence.

As he grew older, he began to feel restless and troubled, striving to formulate a sense of the world around him. He had aimed to find solace in the bustling city life but felt more out of place with each fleeting day.

It was then that he hit upon silence. He found solace in the serenity of the peaks, the delicate rustle of the breeze through the trees, and the calming music of the streams dripping downstream.

He began spending more time in nature and found it to be a haven from the hustle and bustle of the city. He soon realised that it was in these eternities of extensive stillness that he found transparency and stability.

The boy had found his peace in the silent embrace of nature. Afterwards, he returned home and saw a woman walking down the road. She had a big smile and seemed to be having a great time.

As his eye contacted, she glanced at him and smiled even more. It was apparent that she was happy and so was he!

If everyone could be as content as this woman, he realised, everyone would live in harmony. Then he added that her happiness did not indicate that she was without problems.

She was not searching for answers or trying to heal herself; she had no unresolved issues or open wounds. She didn't put forth any effort or expectations; she enjoyed being herself.

So how does that relate to us? How do we achieve happiness without first having our questions answered?

It's simple, really: By practising silence and spreading a smile.

ᐅᐅᐅ

TWENTY

TIME

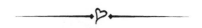

Time was a mysterious creature, ever-changing and unpredictable. It had its impulses and fondness that no one could understand or foresee. Every day, it would move forward, ever-changing, never staying the same.

The story of time was one of cycles and growth. It was about a soul constantly learning and growing through its life excursion. It went through crises and successes, discovering new things along the aisle.

It was a reminder that everyone was connected in ways that could never be fully understood or explained. People came and went through the trek of time, but the equivalent discourses were acquired along the route.

It was an adventure, an acquaintance each person had to go through to recognise their own lives. It was a journey of self-discovery, learning and growing. Time was a reminder to appreciate the moments because they would never return.

Time said it's a gift, one that should never be taken for granted. How hard our life is or the hardships, time is always there to remind us that life goes on. We must make the best of our moments and admire life for what it is.

PASSIONATE LIFE

ᴆᴆᴆ

TWENTY-ONE

UNDERSTAND YOUR UNIQUENESS

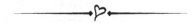

John was a young child who lacked the self-assurance and bravery to face the outside world. He battled to represent himself and feel at ease in any social situation because he was so fearful and standoffish. He was terrified of weakness and was always seeking approval from others.

He decided to take a long walk one day to unwind. He became mindful of something odd in the sky as he was moving. All unexpectedly, a silver moon and thousands of stars appeared in the sky. He had never seen anything more stunning. When John paused and turned to look at the sky, he experienced a sensation of belonging for the first time. The moon and stars seemed to be a part of him.

He felt that he stood out from everyone else in his environment. He had never dreamed of anything like this before. He understood that he possessed abilities and traits that nobody else did. He also realised that no one else could ever be as special as him.

John was overcome by his newly acquired awareness of his individuality. He, at last, understood his significance and what he could contribute to the world. He became more assured and extroverted after that, no longer apprehensive about asserting himself and also being who he was.

It had taken him a long time to realise his uniqueness, but he did. It made him a happier and better person.

Nobody else on the Earth possesses the same perceptions and emotions as you, according to John. It's thrilling to realise each morning that you have no clue what the day will hold. It implies that not even your public persona is like anyone else's. We are all unique, so it's okay if we don't share the same preferences or viewpoints!

So, take a few moments to reflect on how much you appreciate that no twins think the same and how wondrous it is to have such a close connection with others because YOU deserve it. After all, YOU are unique!

ᕰᕰᕰ

TWENTY-TWO

VALUE YOUR VITALITY

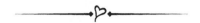

A small ant hill was the home of an ant . The ant was perpetually active, skittering about to gather food, dig new tunnels, and perform other ant-specific tasks.

The ant was working one day when he saw a person passing by. It felt strange when it saw the human. The human's power and vigour astounded the ant. The ant decided to stop and follow the human because it was entranced by it.

It couldn't help but be amazed at the human's incredible abilities as it continued on its journey. It marvelled at the human's flawless ability to carry heavy objects, cover great distances on foot, and perform numerous other tasks.

The ant understood that it was insignificant in comparison to a human. It felt guilty for assuming its own life would always be there. The ant chose to entice itself to intensify its efforts by using its newly acquired admiration for human vitality as inspiration.

It came back to the ant hill and put in even more effort. Every time it felt worn out, it remembered the human and its fortitude, which gave it the stamina to continue.

The ant's perseverance was rewarded. It quickly emerged as the town's most constructive ant. Everyone applauded the ant's endeavours and noted its renewed vigour and vitality.

The ant had taken away a lesson from the human about the value of life. Since that time, the ant has never taken its own life for granted and has worked hard to maximise it.

▷▷▷

TWENTY-THREE

WILLPOWER IS WISDOM

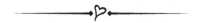

Sam was a young boy who once dreamed of becoming a prosperous entrepreneur. He was highly passionate and enthusiastic but lacked the resolve to follow his dreams. He would constantly find excuses to put off completing his tasks and abandon his plans, leaving him dissatisfied and angry.

Sam once saw an older man looking at the sunset from a bench while strolling the street. Sam halted and inquired as to what the older man was doing. "I am watching the beautiful view and pondering about the power of willpower," the elderly man replied with a smile.

He was curious, asked the man to elaborate. The older man claimed that willpower is an effective ingredient for success. He clarified that willpower is like a muscle that gains power the greater you use it. To accomplish any target, he continued, self-control and focus are crucial.

Sam remembered this guidance, and he started setting manageable objectives that he could accomplish with diligence and focus. He began to form the knack of intervening and stepping outside of his routine. Sam began to see outcomes as he practised this, which gave him more esteem.

Sam achieved his entrepreneurial aspirations and accomplishments thanks to his newly gained willpower. He had become a living example of the force of will and a tribute to the older man's wisdom who had imparted his words of knowledge.

This experience serves as a reminder of the value of willpower in achieving success in life. It is a valuable tool that can support us in achieving our objectives and realising our dreams.

ᗰᗰᗰ

TWENTY-FOUR

XENAS

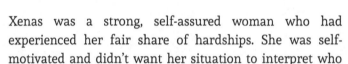

Xenas was a strong, self-assured woman who had experienced her fair share of hardships. She was self-motivated and didn't want her situation to interpret who she was.

She had a quick wit and a contagious giggle that helped to tempt her way out of tough circumstances quite frequently. She also had her pals' backs in everything and was completely devoted to them.

Xenas never shied away from confrontation but was always up for the challenge. She wouldn't let anyone get in the way of her relentless pursuit of being the better representation of herself.

One day, She boldly decided to apply for a position she was interested in. She wasn't sure if she had the knowledge or skills for it, but she was committed to giving it everything she had. She was hired after a long and tricky interview session.

When She achieved her goal, everyone was astounded, and she realised she had chosen wisely. She was ecstatic that her perseverance and hard work had paid off, and she was confident to seize this new opportunity to the fullest.

Despite all the obstacles, She was a strong woman who was ascertained to succeed. She was a guiding light to all of us and a force to be reckoned with.

ᗡᗡᗡ

TWENTY-FIVE

YARE YOUR YEARN

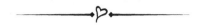

One stormy night, A sudden shift in attitude struck the young man, who had been leading a good life. A strong desire to change things and make a disparity came over him.

The young man's name was Evans, and he had spent the previous year residing in a small town with his family. He was a caring and compassionate man who never hesitated to lend a hand to those in need.

He made the decision to serve as a street volunteer, giving out food to animals and offering consolation to those in need.

He began working as a volunteer at a nearby shelter the following day. He assisted with cleaning the cages, feeding the animals, and providing them affection and company. Initially, some onlookers were perplexed about why he was aiding living creatures when so many folks were genuinely needy. He persisted, though, working every day.

Another day, a homeless man came up to Evans and expressed gratitude for his generosity. This man's life had improved thanks partly to him, who became aware of his contribution.

Day after day, he volunteered his time to ensure that the animals received care, food, and love. He quickly formed a connection with the animals and took care of them.

By yaring his yearning, Evans became a role model for his friends. He demonstrated to them that one could change the world. He revealed to them the power of even seemingly insignificant deeds of generosity.

ᐅᐅᐅ

TWENTY-SIX

ZAPPY ZEN

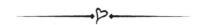

There used to be a senior citizen named Zappy Zen. He was a wonderful and selfless wise person who never hesitated to lend a hand to those in need.

He was renowned for having a calm and nonviolent demeanour. People were happy and hopeful everywhere he went. Life for him was about gratefulness and inner peace rather than wealth or excellence.

A small tourist group visited his town one day. They were seeking a quiet spot to unwind and rest. When they enquired, Zappy Zen smiled and offered them accommodation and as much food as they wanted.

He astonished and moved the travellers with his generosity. They questioned him on how he managed to be so content and joyful. Joy and fulfilment come from within; Zappy Zen responded by saying. Instead of concentrating on material possessions and outer success, pay attention to the little things and good deeds that make life worthwhile.

His words enthralled the travellers, who praised him for his insight. They visited Zappy Zen every day after that, seeking his counsel and insight.

As word of the travellers' experiences spread, visitors worldwide began to arrive at him. He was well-known for his serenity and generosity, which motivated others to discover their inner serenity and happiness.

Thus, Zappy Zen's legend endures and serves as a constant reminder that true happiness comes from within.

ᗞᗞᗞ